What This Book Will Do for You

By the time you've finished reading this book, you will be able to explain stress as your own reaction to situations, your interpretation of experience. You'll be able to identify the factors in your life to which you respond with stress, and you'll be able to take "first aid" measures for reducing the effects of stress and take steps for getting control over the worlds (inner as well as outer) to which you respond with stress. So read on . . .

Other Titles in the Successful Office Skills Series

Rhonda

managing STRESS

DONALD H. WEISS

amacom

AMERICAN MANAGEMENT ASSOCIATION

Library of Congress Cataloging-in-Publication Data

Weiss, Donald H., 1936–
    Managing stress.
    (The Successful office skills series)
    Includes index.
    1. Job stress. I. Title. II. Series.
HF5548.85.W39   1987   158.7   86-47825
ISBN 0-8144-7673-2 (pbk.)

Printing number

10 9 8 7 6 5 4

CONTENTS

Introduction

Good Stress and Bad

S T R E S S ! The word reverberates in your head. Some situations warrant that kind of alarm. When you experience them, you feel bad—*di*stressed.

In other situations, stress receives a bad rap, as they say. Not all stress situations are bad, and some should be invited—situations that produce enjoyment or motivate you to accomplish your most important goals.

During some stressful situations, you feel good, as in the case of a reunion with a close relative or friend whom you haven't seen in many years—what is termed *Eustress,* as opposed to the first kind, *Distress.* Regardless of whether it's good or bad, Eustress or Distress, we can't eliminate or avoid stress altogether.

When something happens, you react to it, you get excited. The stress is *part of your reaction* to the situation, part of your interpretation of the events in the situation. Only the dead can't react to the world around them or inside themselves.

Besides, Distress plays an important part in your life. It's your mind and body's way of preparing to protect you from danger, either by fighting against it or by fleeing from it. Without some stressful situations, you couldn't get your job done or advance in your career. No, rather than get rid of or avoid stress altogether, you need to learn how to manage your stress reactions and the conditions that induce them.

You Produce the Stress

Think about the last time you won a prize. Your heart beat faster, your muscles tensed, you flushed and felt warm, especially in the face and ears. Great fun, yet

1

your bodily reactions during Eustress didn't differ from any you've had during Distress.

Your *body* responds to the situation first. Take, for example, hearing a noise or catching a glimpse of movement out of the corner of your eye. You tense up and feel stress responses, until your mind gets into gear and takes *a second look*. The sound, the glimpse—a friend entering the room quietly. You relax, but the momentary bodily stress produces a mild anger. "Please don't do that again."

On the other hand, let's say the intruder isn't friendly. Then your mind echoes your body's reaction and shouts, "Feet, do your thing!" Or, "Put up your dukes and fight!"

Whether an experience seems good or bad to you depends on how you interpret it. Suppose the stealthy intruder means you no good. You might feel fear. On the other hand, someone else might welcome the confrontation and find it exhilarating rather than frightening. What scares one person may not scare another.

No two people respond to the same situation in the same way. In fact, it's inaccurate to refer to the "same" situation when talking about two people. Each person sees the world differently and responds to it differently. Your beliefs, values, and attitudes are the eyes through which you see the world.

Some people relish danger: mountain climbers, cliff scalers, sky divers, alligator wrestlers, would-be Indiana Joneses. Danger's their business, a challenge. While their bodies undergo stress reactions, their minds thrive on the danger itself. They don't see it as distressing. How about you?

If you're like most people, you read about those daredevils or watch them on TV, but you're unlikely to put yourself into such wonderfully stressful situations. Most people prefer to play it safe, take small risks—like driving to and from work on a crowded freeway.

At the other extreme, some people react with life-threatening stress to situations most others would happily welcome. Asthmatics, for example, often experience breathing difficulty just thinking about something exciting or fun. Their discomfort frightens them, and they go into an attack. The Eustress turns into Distress.

In short, *the events themselves are neutral.* Yet everyone experiences things he or she considers threatening in some manner or another, on the job or off. If the events themselves aren't threatening, then the stress must come from something else.

> *It's our ability, or lack of it, to cope with events and with our reactions to them that generates the stress.*

Therefore, for the remainder of this book, I'm talking about Distress mostly and how to control your worlds (inner as well as outer) to which you respond with stress. It's not *what* happens to you that makes a difference to your life; it's *what you do with what happens* that matters.

Chapter 1

Everyday Stress

You don't have to wrestle alligators to put yourself at risk. Some people risk stress-induced illness, even death, by making excessive demands on themselves in daily living. They're overachievers—aggressive, demanding, hard-driving, short-tempered workaholics.

And I'm not talking only about men—sometimes called Type *A* personalities. I'm including the women Dr. Harriet Braiker labels Type *E*.* These overachieving people drive themselves nearly to death—in part, according to Dr. Braiker, out of a fear of dependency. She also says that Type *E* women are becoming as commonplace as Type *A* men.

*Dr. Harriet B. Braiker, "The Stress of Success: A Special Message for High Achieving Women," in *Working Woman* (August 1986), pp. 63–67, 108–110.

Unwilling to delegate, sometimes contemptuous of less ambitious people, Type *E* women and their Type *A* male analogs compulsively invite every possible job— at work and through civic or social organizations—in order to fill every moment with what they call productive activity. They don't relate well to other people, they often reject the love offered to them, and they rarely give love to others. Lonely and frequently exhausted, they substitute even more work or activity for companionship, and they literally run themselves into the ground.

So, you see, you really don't have to wrestle alligators to put your life at risk due to stress. On the other hand, though we run into Type *A* and Type *E* people more frequently than we do alligator wrestlers, they still constitute a small, neurotic-compulsive population when compared with the rest of us ordinary, everyday types. We usually find ourselves at risk even when we're not looking for it.

> *We feel the greatest amount of stress when we feel or believe ourselves powerless to control, affect, or alter the situation in which we find ourselves or when we run up against something unexpected over which we're unprepared to exercise control.*

Take Donna Smith. A 38-year-old meeting planner working as an account manager with an incentive travel company, Donna thought her job was threatened because for the second time in four months, a program for the same client, Electronics Industries, seemed to be blowing up.

Activities the client thought would be held during the company's four-day sales-recognition conference (such as track-and-field games) weren't incorporated into the contract written by the sales department and signed by the client. Party sites (such as the hotel's pool for a reception) were apparently discussed but not included in the final signed letter or agreement.

In addition, the hotel the client chose couldn't put up all the company's VIPs in suites. The costing department also understated everything, and there was no

4

way Donna could bring the program in under the negotiated price, which was what Ellen, her boss, expected of her. And to top it off, the guests were a week behind on their reservations. The same sorts of problems had popped up during Donna's first crack at managing Electronics Industries' incentive program.

Everyone was upset with the account manager—the client, the sales department, Donna's boss, and Donna herself. Everyone was angry with her in spite of the fact that all these foul-ups either occurred before she took over or were happening at the client's end.

The mother of two girls, aged 11 and 13, Donna was married to an engineer. She had no compelling economic reason for working, but her job was important to her. As the first woman in her family to graduate from college (after she sent her second child off to school), she wanted a career for herself. However, Stan, her husband, saw no reason for her to work outside the home.

He often poked fun at her job ("baby-sitting a bunch of partiers"). He resented the two or three nights each week that she worked until seven or eight o'clock. He fought against her out-of-town trips (sometimes for two weeks at a time, spaced approximately one and a half months apart). He disliked her constant state of agitation, her exhaustion, her distance. In rebellion, he helped no more than was absolutely necessary, even to the point of refusing to hire a full-time housekeeper when she asked for one.

The way Stan saw it, if things became tough enough, Donna would quit. "It's not the money," he claimed. "It's the principle. She should stay home or get a job that takes less time and energy—like a secretary or something."

Regardless of how it looks, Donna's was not a case of what some people call the superwoman syndrome—women who try to do too much to *prove* themselves in spite of a lack of support or help. While Donna's lifestyle approximated that syndrome, she was like most other people—just trying to make a career for herself and do her job the best she could. Rather than attempting to be a superwoman, she was simply caught up in the turmoil of management, both in her job and at home.

Most career wives/mothers, such as Donna, do deal effectively with almost all of what they go through (as some recent studies show). In many cases, they get the support and help they need from their families, and these women cope with their stresses better than many women who work only in the home. Whether it's the support or help they get that gives them the strength to handle their lives, or it's something in their personality that led them to work outside the home in the first place, no one seems to know.

For the most part, Donna found Stan's attitudes more amusing than threatening, she took things as they came, and she felt pretty comfortable with herself. She, too, coped with the demands made on her. Of course, much of what she called coping consisted of smoking two packs of cigarettes a day and drinking two or three stiff vodka tonics a night to prepare for bed.

She exercised once a week at the supermarket, she amused herself by poring over trade magazines or helping the girls with their homework. She nourished herself with a bowl of sugar-coated cereal for breakfast, a fried hamburger with french fries for lunch, and a frozen potpie for dinner—that is, when she had time for dinner.

Donna coped, in her way. The problems with the Electronics Industries program might not have thrown her this way, either, if Ellen hadn't fired four other account managers since the first of the year. Donna not only faced a threat to her competency and self-esteem—she feared for her job. Almost everything coming at her seemed to her to be beyond her control.

No matter what she did, she felt helpless to repair the damage everyone else did to this program. Since she took the heat from everyone involved in the snafus, she blamed herself, as well. She thought: "I just can't negotiate properly. I'm not aggressive enough. If I really knew what I was doing, I could put things right. I guess I just don't have it and should get out now before I'm fired. Maybe Mother and I can open a boutique or something."

In her mind, the problems with the program could destroy her career, everything she'd worked to accomplish. She saw herself at great personal risk and felt that she faced it alone.

_____

The Stresses of Home-Based Employment

Stay-at-home workers have their own stresses. The same recent studies mentioned in the text show that many stay-at-home workers have greater difficulty coping with their stressful situations than do out-of-the-home workers, due only in part to emotional differences between the two types of workers.

_____

Not one to complain or to "unload" on anyone, Donna felt further inhibited from talking out her problems by Stan's attitudes. She hardly talked to him at all, about anything, and when she did, she appeared distant, tense, and unfriendly.

Stan, in turn, feared his plan would backfire on him: Instead of quitting and staying home, Donna was getting angry with him and might leave him. Though he'd much rather she work than leave, he was locked into his attitudes and couldn't make the first overtures. Afraid that an open discussion could precipitate a separation, he wouldn't confront the issues either. Instead of reaching out, he clammed up as well. Neither of them knew what to do.

In case you think Donna's a figment of my imagination, consider these sobering facts. Today, as more women advance into management, stress-related diseases are killing them, too. They're catching up with men in frequency of heart attacks, and they're having them at an earlier age than women used to. Lung cancer now exceeds breast cancer as a killer of women.

Actually, you should recognize Donna easily. That's why I gave you as much background as I did. She's just another working stiff like you and me.

Though I've based parts of her life on that of a close friend, Donna's not just one woman. She's many women. She's also many men. She's a composite drawn from my years as a counselor/trainer that represents typical men and women caught up in the whirl of *ordinary daily living.* Ordinary daily living puts most folks at risk.

The Donnas of the world—men as well as women (and not just the extreme Type *E*'s and *A*'s or superwomen)—have to learn how to control their stress through *self*-management, and how to gain control over their worlds and their own actions through goal-directed knowledge.

Chapter 2

What Stresses You?

Before you can use self-management to control your stress, you have to identify *what* you're trying to control—the conditions that induce stress (called *stressors*).

Leave aside the death of a loved one, a divorce—personal tragedies of those sorts. Though such situations induce the greatest amount of stress for most people, focus instead on situations in which you find yourself during most of your waking hours—in work or work-related activities, including the trip to and from the job. Anything said about controlling reactions to daily happenings applies as well to controlling reactions to personal tragedies.

Since your response (your interpretation) determines what the situation means to you, instead of my listing a number of so-called stressful situations and asking you to rate them, you examine your own experiences and decide when you feel the greatest amount of stress—for example, frequent interruptions by co-workers, demands made on you by your supervisor, tasks you feel inadequate to perform, a performance review.

A racing heart, tense muscles, and so on signal the presence of any kind of stress, and the frequent or continual presence of those physical reactions produces damaging effects. I've listed below some of the most common of these effects. You can use the list to begin your evaluation. Check off those effects you've experienced often or experience now.

____	1. Fatigue.
____	2. Insomnia.
____	3. Distraction.
____	4. Guilt feelings.
____	5. Indecision.
____	6. A lack of interest in or caring for other people, sex, or other types of recreation.
____	7. Short temper.
____	8. Impatience with yourself and others.
____	9. A feeling of being pressured by the demands of others on you.
____	10. A desire to escape from everything and everyone (often by using alcohol or other drugs).
____	11. Being afraid of dying, yet having thoughts of suicide.

Taken one at a time, the symptoms on the list may not indicate serious stress, they usually pose no danger, and are easily diagnosed and corrected. However, having several of those feelings or thoughts simultaneously or for any significant length of time can signal severe Distress—Distress that can produce silent hypertension, painful ulcers or coronary disease, cardiac arrest, severe allergies, skin problems, some forms of cancer, and other diseases too often dismissed as "all in your head."

You now need a chart of conditions under which you feel stress. Use the one below to help you outline what

are for you the most common stressful situations. Start
by recognizing the feelings you experience fairly regularly.

In the first column, identify your most frequent feelings, then indicate how often you feel them and which
of them you felt most recently. Don't worry about order
or about analyzing them. Associate freely, using pencil
and paper, with my examples as a guide. When you
make your own chart, leave the last column blank and
leave several lines between each feeling. You'll fill
them in later.

Do the exercise now. You'll get much more out of this
book once you have that outline. You'll be using it, and
other devices, to help you get better control over your
stress.

FEELING	HOW OFTEN	WHEN	WHAT
My face flushes	Several times a day	Every day	
My muscles tense	Several times a day	Every day	
Insomnia	Several nights a month	Last week	
Fatigue	Every night	After work	

Now complete the last column. Identify the circumstances you associate with your feelings. Follow three
different steps.

First, describe the experience as objectively as you
can, in terms of mere facts. Don't use emotionally
loaded or evaluative words. I'll illustrate how to do it
with Donna's situation:

*Phil—the client's representative—asked me why
the reception wouldn't be at the pool.*

Second, describe your interpretations of the experience. Associate emotions and values with your feelings.

I flushed [feeling] *when he asked me about it. I
felt angry* [emotion].

Third, analyze those interpretations. Explain what
made you feel that way.

10

I felt angry because Phil called me incompetent when I said the pool hadn't been written into the contract, shouting at me when I told him the reception was to be held at the gazebo area.

Use Donna's statements as models for your own: (1) a statement of fact, (2) a description of your feelings and emotions, and (3) an explanation of why you felt that way. Once you do this part of the exercise, I'm going to ask you a question that will help put many of your stressful experiences into perspective. You'll be better able to answer that question if you complete the exercise first.

Chapter 3

First Steps Toward Self-Management

Knowing what your stress reactions are and under what circumstances you feel them only begins the process of self-management. Now you need to know what to do about them if you don't want to feel them or if you think they're threatening to you. And since not all stress reactions are bad, you *may* want to figure out ways to *repeat* them.

First, put your experiences into perspective by answering this question.

What is the worst possible thing that could ever happen to me?

Here's what I'm after. When asked this question, Donna answered that an incapacitating stroke frightens her more than anything else. Living death, it's called. Lying on her back, staring out into a world with which she can't communicate. A living consciousness in a damaged brain and an unmoving body.

Now, you answer that question, in writing.

Next, if you can do it, try to visualize your worst possible thing in your mind's eye. Try to live it— whether it's to die or to be paralyzed or to lose a loved one or whatever it may be, unless it's just too horrible a prospect for you.

I don't mean for you to say blandly, "It would be like going to sleep," or "It would be very lonely"—or to look at it as if you were a third-party observer. Rather, try to simulate your situation vividly. If it's death, try blocking out as much sensation as you can. If it's the loss of a loved one, try feeling the loneliness. Let Donna illustrate again.

With her eyes closed, in her imaginary stroke, Donna feels herself lying in a bed, her head and shoulders propped up on pillows, and she sees out through a door into a hospital corridor where people walk back and forth past her room. Some of them glance in, but no one stops to talk, and she can't call out to them.

In her visualization, Donna feels no physical pain, but everything stops for her except her ability to see and to hear, to think and to feel, to wish and to wait for death. She's locked up in her head like a clam in its shell. For Donna, nothing is as terrible.

At this point, Donna had to ask herself, "Are Phil's attitude and behavior the worst possible thing that could happen to me?" Her answer's obvious.

When Phil blamed her, even though in fact she had no control over the situation, she became very stressed, partly because at that time she failed to use this little trick for putting the situation into perspective. By comparing the reception-site problem with her imagined stroke, she calmed herself and, thinking clearly again, realized that the pool simply wasn't specified in the contract as the reception site. She had nothing to do with writing the agreement, and she bore no responsibility for the oversight.

Somewhere along the way, it had gotten fixed in Phil's mind that they would have the reception at the pool—probably when he and Bruce, the salesman, made the site visit together. Donna wasn't sure, but they may have been talking about the reception when they walked through the pool area.

When (and if) you do the exercise, you may cry or feel distressed. Don't be alarmed. Stay calm and remember you're just vividly imagining the experience. It's not real.

If you did the exercise, you probably found it difficult. You may have experienced some pain, for which I'm sorry, but the pain gives you a basis for making the comparison between the worst possible thing that could happen to you and the experiences you've identified in your chart.

To put your stress situations into perspective, ask:

Is anything on my list the worst thing that could ever happen to me?

When something happens—your supervisor yells at you, you miss a deadline, you get caught in a traffic jam on the way to work—compare it with your worst possible thing. Nothing seems as terrible, and the stress you momentarily felt goes away.

Don't worry. You don't have to go through an ordeal every time you feel stress. Instead, here's another way of dealing with it.

Decide which feelings you want to keep and which you want at least to reduce. Look again at what you called the causes of your stress—in step three of the analysis you did earlier—and generalize by answering two sets of questions.

In the past, what did I do in that type of situation? What did I do to handle my feelings? What did I do to repeat or avoid that sort of situation?

When you answer those questions, you'll have a better understanding of what you've done this time to allow yourself to feel stress—Eustress as well as Distress. You'll see how you coped, or didn't cope, with the situations and/or your own feelings. Then ask the next set of questions.

When those situations arise again, what can I do to repeat the feelings I want to keep or eliminate those I don't want, or at least reduce their impact or intensity?

Answering those questions starts you planning ways for getting control over yourself and therefore over your stress. In the remainder of this book, I'll describe three principal ways of developing self-management skills for dealing with stress: first aid, altering the environment (including your relationships with other people), and planning for your life.

Chapter 4

First Aid for Stress

No one calls ordinary, normal, and unavoidable stress an illness or a disease. At the same time, just as pain signals an organic, skeletal, muscular, or neural problem, stress signals an environmental problem. Unlike pain, however, severe stress that interferes with your life won't respond to two aspirins and bed rest. Rather, everyone has to find his or her remedy of choice—the one method, or combination of methods, that works best for him or her.

Usually, people respond well to methods that don't involve expensive equipment (as in electronic biofeedback) or special places (such as spas or exercise centers) or trained professionals (such as psychotherapists). Crying or yelling, stretching, physical exercise, dancing, sex, listening to music, light reading, moderate drinking, stroking a pet, meditation, or hypnosis— each method helps, but only you can decide which works for you.

Exercises to Reduce Stress

When you experience stress as tension, you feel a need to reduce that stress. In first aid for stress, you do something different from the situation that induces the stress—something that doesn't induce stress and/or has a chemical effect on the brain that reduces the tension—and you feel better.

First aid exercises or activities work because the brain can't concentrate on two things at the same time. Each major center of the brain controls one and only one set of sensations or feelings or functions, and they respond to different types of activities in only their particular way. The brain flashes back and forth between one experience and another, but it can't consciously focus on both simultaneously.

First aid exercises, even just basic stretching exercises, also work because they produce a bodily sensation that registers in your brain as a sense of well-being. Bodily sensations affect feelings and attitudes. When you feel good, especially when you feel good about yourself, the world around you looks good, as well.

Research discloses that crying helps because tears remove irritants, chemicals that are clinically associated with stress. Once they're removed, you feel better. Going off by yourself and having a good cry for a few minutes can relieve your tension. And, men, forget that old saw that real men don't cry. That may be one reason why the "real men" who don't cry don't live as long as the real women who do.

Yelling has a similar effect. Though it doesn't remove irritants from the nervous system unless accompanied by crying, it releases the stress by giving vent to your feelings. Screaming at no one in particular, and in the privacy of your own room or car or some other solitary place, calms you and gives you a chance to attack the situation rationally later.

A number of nonstrenuous exercises relax muscles and provide some relief from stress. In the simplest, with your feet spread apart slightly, bend over and touch your toes, or come as close to them as you can, keeping your knees straight as you reach downward and bending them as you straighten up. If you touch your toes easily, reach for the floor between your feet, hands flat. Do this three times. It stretches, loosens, and relaxes the muscles in your lower back, in your shoulders, and in your legs.

An exercise that can be done in three different ways provides relaxation for the whole body. In the first way, lie flat on any surface—your bed, your floor, your desktop (if it's not as cluttered as mine). With arms close to your sides, tighten (contract) every muscle in your body and hold it for a slow count of five. Release. Repeat this three times in rapid succession. Get up and go about your business feeling more relaxed.

Remember both sets of feelings, the tense as well as the relaxed. If after a stress-inducing situation, you feel tension in your muscles, run through this whole body-relaxation exercise. You'll feel better.

Of course, you probably can't lie down on your desk or office floor, but you can do the same exercise a second way: standing next to your desk. With your hands down in front of you, tense your entire body. As you contract your muscles, to the slow count of five, pull your hands out to the sides, maintaining the tension. Release, lowering your arms to the front position again. Three repetitions here, too, provide relaxation from whatever has induced the stress.

The third variation takes a few minutes longer. Either standing or lying down as before, tense each set of muscles one at a time, from your feet to the top of your head. Start by tensing the muscles in your feet. Hold the tension for a quick five count. Still holding the tension in your feet, tense the muscles in your calves and shins for a five count. Holding the tension in your feet, calves and shins, tense the muscles in your thighs—and so on until your whole body is contracted and tense.

Once you reach your head, hold this peak tension for two or three seconds before working your way back down your body, relaxing each set of muscles in the reverse of the sequence you followed in the tensing segment of the exercise. Once you get back down through your feet, lie or stand quietly in this relaxed state for a few seconds and repeat the exercise. Again, three repetitions suffice.

In addition to these isometric exercises, vigorous

exercise satisfies a variety of needs. The activity itself involves *doing* something. Since stress feelings become most intolerable when you feel that you can't do anything about your situation, doing something to reduce the tension releases you from that frustration. That's why some people say to *do anything at all,* even if it's the *wrong* thing.

Exercise, especially aerobic exercise, offers another benefit. It releases chemicals in the brain that relax the whole body—endorphins, the body's own mild anesthetic. They're natural chemicals that kill pain, relax muscles, and create mild thrills or highs in the nervous system. Medical researchers are hard at work to synthesize these chemicals as nonaddictive alternatives to both medicinal and illegal drugs.

Exercise—even jogging or fast walking—bores a lot of people. Many of them do aerobic dancing to relieve their boredom. Yet, as in the case of jogging, aerobic dancing can cause trauma to the feet, ankles, shins, knees, lower back, and women's breasts and reproductive system. You need to take care when getting involved in any vigorous exercise.

Be sure to have a medical checkup first. If you're over 40, include an exercise test (a stress test) in order to spot blood pressure or other coronary disorders that can destroy you during exercise.

Fast dancing, in any form, though in no way a fitness program, can relieve stress temporarily. It's usually very social, it's fun, you can lose yourself in it, and if it's done continuously over a period of 30 minutes or more, dancing can have some of the same aerobic effects as jogging.

Sex Can Help

A corollary to exercise and dancing is sex. Now that's not a come-on. While not recommending promiscuity, I am saying that recreational sex between consenting adults (especially if they care deeply for each other) combines some of the benefits of all the exercises I've just described, plus several of its own.

Sexual stimulation releases the chemical acetylcholine into the brain. The increase of acetylcholine drives the arousal further. The pleasure centers of the brain then dominate everything and block out all other sensations, thoughts, and feelings. As some people have said, the brain is our primary sex organ.

Additionally, recreational sex involves stretching and other physical activities. Even if you don't include dancing as part of the fun, it increases the heart rate for a short period of time. It involves muscle tensing and relaxing, with a strong release that induces sleep most of the time.

Research shows that sex reduces high blood pressure. But besides being good for you, it's fun—especially if you include a partner.

People often underrate the fun side of sex. They equate fulfillment with orgasms. Or they think of it strictly in terms of procreation, often treating it as a divine commandment to go forth and multiply. For them, recreational sex is bad or sinful. Both groups miss out on some of the best experiences you can have with sex.

Recreational sex involves sensuality as well as sexuality. It acts as a stress reducer by producing a sense of well-being, a sense of security, a sense of self-worth, a sense of contentment.

I'm not talking about sexual techniques that delay orgasm, or any of the other sexual fads that induce their own forms of performance anxiety and stress. I'm talking about 30 minutes of what most people enjoy about sensuality, with or without orgasm, before or after orgasm.

Most people enjoy being held close, hugged tightly, caressed gently, rubbed or massaged, stroked on the hair. They enjoy kissing one another softly. Their skin vibrates with nerve endings just waiting to be lightly tickled by fingers, lips, or silky objects. Few people worry about the boss's reaction to their report in the morning when their lovers wrap them in their arms. In fact, why not wake up a little earlier than usual and make tender love before you deliver that report? You'll feel more at ease if you do.

However, when matters get out of hand, as in Donna's case, nothing can take your mind from your stressors. And "nothing" includes sex as well as exercise and dancing.

Music and Reading

Donna uses alcohol to help separate her mind from work-related stress. It's not highly recommended. One or two drinks before bed disconnect brain links and help relax the body. Still, alcohol is a highly addictive depressant. Sparing use. That's all.

A much better alternative to drinking or taking other drugs—including prescription drugs, such as Valium—is listening to soothing music. Pachelbel's Canon in D, Strings, Bach's Air from the Suite No. 3 in D Minor, Albinoni's Adagio in G Minor—soft, gentle, wordless music is among the better-known relaxers.

Lesser known, but becoming more popular, is the music written for electronic instruments such as the synthesizer and other music enhancers—music such as that written and/or performed by Andreas Vollenweider, Daniel Kobialka, and Michel Uyttebroek, among others. Called New Age Jazz, it induces relaxation better than most other music. You can hear it on many public radio stations in at least 37 states. Check with the PBS station in your town to see if and when it broadcasts a program called "Hearts of Space."

Combine listening to music and reading a book. While on a break or at lunch, turn on some relaxing music and pull out a book. At home, sit quietly by yourself. If you have children, read to them. It relaxes you because you lose yourself, and you get in some quality time with the kids—time that gives you a sense of well-being also. Try a novel, nonfiction literature unrelated to your work, or a book of humor—anything in which you can lose yourself for a short time.

Combining light reading and listening to relaxing music with stroking a furry pet affects your heart rate and blood pressure in startling ways. Recent studies have shown that elderly people with pets live more comfortably, suffer fewer so-called old-age disorders, enjoy themselves much more, and live longer than do people without them. And highly excitable people, even violent ones, calm down when they care for animals. Disturbed children sleep better when they cuddle a live creature rather than a stuffed one.

I rarely recommend watching television and, then, only certain programs: very funny sitcoms that don't involve serious social issues as their main thrust. Many satirical shows are funny, but they don't relax you because they replace one set of stressful situations with others. Stick with shows that give you a chance to laugh for the fun of it. And having fun absorbs your mind. You relax.

Meditation and Self-Talk

On the other side of the coin, you can relax by getting serious, too. Meditation (whether religious or secular) removes the stress you're feeling by focusing your mind on something not stressful, on an inspirational thought or a prayer or a monotonous sound (such as a yogic mantra). Visualizing a scene you find beautiful works as well as most meditation. Use music to reinforce the effect. You'll find yourself relaxing very quickly and deeply.

Hypnosis, either self-induced or induced by a professional, is the most radical form of first aid relaxation you can use to gain mental control over stress. Before becoming involved in anything that extreme, try some exercises that border on self-hypnosis.

The first exercise consists of breathing. That's all, but you concentrate on your breathing while doing it. When you feel stress on the job, interrupt your work and do this for five to ten minutes. After practice, you'll get the same benefit from the exercise after *as little as thirty seconds.* Here's what you do.

Find a corner by yourself, preferably in a room with the door closed and the lights dimmed. Sit up straight in a chair, with your hands in your lap and your feet on the floor, or if you can do it, lie down with your arms folded across your chest or resting at your sides.

Tense your whole body and hold it for a slow count of ten; feel and remember the sensation of extreme tension. Let go suddenly (relax your muscles); feel and remember the difference between the sensations of tension and relaxation. You want to achieve the feelings of relaxation.

Now take a deep breath, hold it for a slow count of five, and let go slowly. That's your permission to yourself to relax. Use that signal every time you want to relax.

Breathe naturally. Listen to your breathing; feel it in your nose, throat, and chest; pay attention only to it. If you have trouble concentrating exclusively on your breathing, if other thoughts or feelings creep into your consciousness at the same time as your breathe, say to yourself as you inhale and exhale: "Breathe in," "Breathe out." This *self-talk* helps you concentrate for as long as you continue the exercise (and helps to keep you awake).

Self-talk facilitates relaxation because you respond most positively to your own voice. In self-talk, the person you trust the most tells you what to do. You feel safe giving yourself over to the voice you hear. And you do what you're told more readily when you tell yourself to do it.

Out-loud self-talk is more difficult than the subvocal form. We're taught that only crazy people talk to themselves out loud. While that may be true, self-talk actually helps you keep from going crazy when you're feeling the most stress.

Since you, too, may find it difficult to talk to yourself out loud, I'll tell you later how to do so by using an audiocassette. Now, however, we need to get back to the breathing exercise.

Continue breathing with focused self-awareness for as long as you feel stressed, using self-talk to achieve the best concentration. As you do the exercise, your eyes will probably close of their own accord. Let them. After five or ten minutes, you should feel comfortable enough to open your eyes slowly, enjoying the feeling of relaxation.

Take care not to nod off to sleep. The exercise is designed to allow you to relax before sleeping, to give you a better night's sleep *after* you've done it. So use the exercise when you retire as well as at work; then roll over and go to sleep.

The next exercise will help you sleep better, especially if you're experiencing as much stress as Donna, but you can also use it in the office. It requires more time than the breathing exercise, and you should do it in the quiet of a closed room (if you can). It's called total relaxation.

Prepare for this exercise the same way you do for the breathing exercise. If possible, put on some music. Then do the breathing exercise for about one or two minutes.

As you breathe, visualize in your mind's eye the sort of setting in which you feel most content. See yourself there—lying on the warm sands of a beach, on the top of a hill, in the warm, soft grass, or swinging in a hammock. Use your creative imagery to watch the clouds drift lazily across the sky. Feel the sun warm your skin. Let the warmth fill your mind and body.

Once you are deep into your visualization, instruct your body to relax—one set of muscles at a time, from the top of your head to your feet, the way you did in an earlier exercise. Periodically quit directing your muscles and allow yourself to rest quietly on your beach or hilltop or wherever else your mind has taken you.

If you lose concentration at any point, return to your breathing exercise. Use self-talk to regain your concentration.

When you've worked all the way down to your feet, lie or sit quietly for a few minutes before opening your eyes, counting to ten slowly as you do. Continue resting for a few minutes before moving about again. You'll be very relaxed, and you have to give your brain a chance to recover before forcing it back into the real world.

Some people have difficulty relaxing unless they hear a voice tell them what to do throughout the exercise. That, however, is not self-management. Using a professionally produced audiocassette tape permits someone else to manage you. Though you could focus your mind on a nonstressful message spoken by another person, you get more effective results when you feel in full control of yourself.

Make a tape of your own voice telling you to relax and how to do it. Use the script in Appendix A as the basis for creating your own. Read your script into a recorder, speaking softly, slowly, and lovingly. This is your tape, designed to speak to you, to help you take care of your own relaxation problems. Turn it on whenever you find yourself having an intense stress reaction over which you can't seem to get control.

All these exercises and other stress-reduction methods are first aid, at best. They give only temporary and superficial relief. Whatever you do, the conditions that induced the stress are still there. You might compare doing these activities to giving a painkiller to someone with a broken leg.

They help you most when you feel some type of tension and you can't get control over the conditions that induce it. You then take control over the *one thing over which you can get complete control: your own reactions.* When you're relaxed, reason prevails. You can then tackle the conditions that induced the stress in the first place.

Chapter 5

Controlling Conditions That Produce Stress

Of all the conditions that induce stress, you have greatest control over those you produce yourself, such as poor eating habits and poor sleeping habits.

Poor Eating Habits

Junk-food junkies, that's what most people have become. Sugar, salt, grease, caffeine—the main ingredients in junk food—all damage your internal organs and nervous system. Sugar's an abrasive, as far as your nervous system's concerned. So is caffeine. Salt and grease clog more than drains. They clog your arteries, as well, and angina's no fun.

No matter what the commercials tell you, caffeine doesn't help you relax. It does just the opposite. It seems that few people can put in a day's work without coffee, tea, or colas. (By the way, I sin along with the worst of them when it comes to coffee.) The more stressful the day, the more caffeine you're likely to consume. The effect simply intensifies the stress feelings. You'd think we would see that by now and cut back on whatever it is we drink.

At the same time, a great number of people eat foods destined to kill them—fatty beef, rich creams, bacon and eggs, among many others. Very few people learn much about nutrition, not even many physicians. Instead, most people allow the sirens of mass media to lure them into the fast-food joints that serve up fried chicken, fried hamburgers, fried potatoes, fried onion rings, and fried pies. And of course, they wash it all down with—you guessed it—a sugar-filled soft drink or a cup of coffee or a frosty mug of beer. They pack on weight while getting little nourishment from what they eat. They then feel stress from being overweight and receive little help from their own bodies in dealing with that stress.

Nutritionists tell us that foods rich in protein energize. Foods with high concentrations of complex carbohydrates calm us down.

When you feel energized, situations don't seem to be as overwhelming. A diet of low-fat meats, such as chicken or turkey, fish, and many different types of beans (especially soya) will give you the energy you need just as well as beef, without all the fat.

Be sure that you don't eat protein-rich foods before going to bed or when trying to unwind. Take some carbohydrates instead (crackers, milk, fruit, or vegetables). They tend to calm people, counteracting the protein they've ingested all day.

By eating a high-protein breakfast and a high-protein lunch (unless your doctor has warned you against it for some specific health reason unique to you), you'll have the strength to cope with your work world. Eat a light dinner, one high in complex carbohydrates if you don't expect to do anything strenuous afterward. If you must snack at night (and most people, it seems, must), make it light and also high in complex carbohydrates. You'll feel better—and you'll probably lose weight in the process.

Dieting

Dieting is sometimes a symptom of stress. Feel fat? Diet. Dieting itself produces stress, and since the act of eating reduces anxiety, you eat more. Diet gurus get rich on *fat stress*.

Losing weight has become an American obsession. As a result, some people have developed neurotic habits, such as anorexia nervosa (which may result in starving yourself to death). If you look bad—and today that means fat, soft, flabby—you feel guilt as well as stress. To overcome the guilt, some people let themselves get fatter, which then produces more stress. And if they don't do anything about it, they could hurt themselves physically. Rather than feel stressed over your weight, eating less of everything will accomplish your goal.

Bona fide nutritionists will tell you, if it's published in a popular book (as opposed to a reputable, but boring, reference book), don't bother. At best, it won't help much; at worst, it can harm you. Check with your physician before going on any diet.

Poor Sleeping Habits

Overall, it's best not to eat or exercise before going to sleep. Your body works hard when it digests food, and it gets revved up from the exercise.

Some people toss and turn all night. Some sit up to watch the same late show for the umpteenth time. Others party till the milkman's hour. The lack of sleep saps them of vital energy, and that loss of energy interferes with their performance on the job. Both the loss of energy and the interference with performance produce stress.

No one has clearly identified just how sleep reenergizes the system, but it does. Sleep is crucial to your ability to cope with your ordinary daily stresses. Without it, you lack the energy you need, you feel incapable of dealing with your problems. When you suffer from serious sleep deprivation, you feel totally out of control. The more out of control you feel, the more stressed you feel. And the cycle goes round and round.

When you, like Donna, find yourself working all day and then doing chores until late at night, you can still get a good, if not long, night's sleep by doing at least three of the following four things.

First, before you prepare for bed, sit quietly in a comfortable chair and listen to soft music. If someone's with you, talk quietly about something pleasant. If no one's there, read and listen to music. Take at least 20 minutes to unwind.

Second, take a warm bath or shower. If you have a massage shower head, play it up and down your back, over your head and shoulders, up and down the sides of your neck. If you soak in a tub of hot water, turn the lights low (use candles if you don't have a dimmer switch), listen to soft music (from a radio or stereo in another room, unless you have a waterproof portable), and come out of it before the water turns cold. If you have a hot tub or jacuzzi, spend no more than 20 minutes in it.

If you're still feeling a little stressed, do a third thing—one of the relaxation exercises I described earlier. You can skip this step if the resting and the tub or shower have left you as limp as they leave some people. Otherwise, do it.

Fourth, if you're with a lover, make love. If you've been very stressed, it's best to keep it short but sweet, with the emphasis on the latter. A boisterously good time will have the same energizing effect that exercise has. Instead of sleeping, you'll feel more awake—and probably hungry. Eating on top of everything else will only make matters worse.

If there's no one there with whom to make love, and you're still feeling even a little stressed after the shower or bath, you can try other things. Some people find satisfaction from masturbation, but if you have any inhibitions about it, it will only induce stress for you. If that's the case, don't do it. Instead, do the relaxation exercise that works best for you.

Controlling Your Physical World

Not only do modern Americans assault themselves with junk food and poor sleeping habits, they live in an environment where physical factors can affect emotional well-being.

One such factor is the *air,* both outside and indoors. Dirty air creates breathing difficulties, which in turn, frighten people suffering from respiratory problems or heart disease. Sometimes you don't know what's wrong, and your inability to breathe comfortably scares you even more. You can't take the right corrective action when you don't know what the problem is. Not taking control creates stress.

Check out the air in your office or plant. Is the system circulating clean air and circulating it thoroughly? If it's not, have it overhauled by a competent technician.

On very hot days, check with the weather center in your community about pollutants in the air. Particles of dirt and injurious chemicals are more tolerable in cool or cold temperatures than they are during hot weather, but only up to certain levels. The level of dangerous ozone (heavy oxygen) also increases in hot weather. Especially if you suffer from a respiratory problem, hypertension, or heart disease, take it easy when these pollutants are high. Otherwise, you'll feel great stress, which only makes matters worse.

Light is another factor that can affect you emotionally. Proper lighting reduces stress. When you can't clearly see what you're doing, you can expect to feel stress. If you stare at a computer screen all day, you can expect eyestrain-induced stress. Eyestrain caused by a need to get glasses or to correct a prescription simply compounds the problem.

Very dim light and overly bright light alike have negative effects. A lighting expert should be called in if a number of people are experiencing unexplainable headaches and/or eyestrain.

Excessively bright light produces glare that induces stress. Especially after a long, hard day, when you return home from work, keep the house light soft, dimmer than what you experienced at work. That helps you wind down. And don't do relaxation exercises or sleep in a bright light, if you can avoid it. It's self-defeating.

Sound also plays an important role in governing emotions. City dwellers live in a noisy world, made even nosier by contemporary tastes in music. You have little control over city noises. You can close windows (if the place is air-conditioned). You can enclose machines (if they're small enough and you don't jeopardize safety or restrict access to them). But you do have full control over the volume of the radio or stereo to which you're listening. Loud sound, even musical sound, creates stress.

Loud music is energizing. It's great for fast dancing or for marching. When you're trying to come down from daily stresses, or if you need to induce calm in the work environment, use soft music. People may kid around a lot about how bad elevator music is, but they're really not supposed to *listen* to it. It's designed to blend into the background of their world, keeping it calm and relaxed. If you work in a noisy factory, wear those earplugs. They'll save more than your hearing. Keep the workplace quiet, and you'll cut back on at least one more condition that induces stress.

I have to throw in a caveat here. In my own experience with young people tuned in to their own cultural values (loud music as well as funny-looking clothing), asking them to work in a quiet, relaxed atmosphere may make them feel more stress. Unless quiet is required by the work itself, or unless their music disrupts a large part of your workforce or disturbs a number of other people, let them listen to whatever pleases them. If quiet benefits the greatest number, encourage them to buy a little, portable radio to which they can listen through a headset.

Other parts of the physical world impact on us and induce stress, but those I've discussed play a paramount role. Look around. Analyze the world in which you work and live. What aspects of it can you change to make it less stressful for you?

Chapter 6

Stress in Your Relationships

Jean Paul Sartre, the French existentialist playwright, believed that hell is living with other people. Donna can relate to that. For her, even if she controlled the physical factors in her world, and cut back on her smoking and coffee drinking, she'd still have the same people problems that pretty nearly brought her to the brink. Only by controlling her relationships with others did she get control over her stress.

As is the case with stress in general, you can sometimes benefit from Distress induced by interpersonal relations. Creativity, innovation, problem solving all benefit from tensions between people, if they handle the disagreements constructively.

Donna started with the contract with Electronics Industries, since that's where most of the problems she'd encountered originated. She handled that by calling in Bruce, the sales rep, and the hotel representative to deal with the client managers' misperceptions of what they were supposed to get. Any debate over the contract was between them.

Since the costing department understated costs to the client on the contract as written, Donna referred the fact that she couldn't come in under the negotiated price back to her boss, Ellen. She delegated the problem upward for the *department manager* to handle. Donna does what she can to hold down prices, but she doesn't demand miracles of herself anymore.

As for Stan's attitudes, she doesn't demand miracles from him, either. Still, she had to confront him rather than let the situation at home, with regard to her career, fester. The longer Donna and Stan stayed silent, the worse the situation became and the more stress they both experienced. Her work outside the home really isn't their main problem. It's their inability to communicate with each other about it that's destroying their marriage.

As with any other attempt to manage stress, there's a relatively simple method that's hard to implement. It's called a *feedback session.* In the session, you tell other people what you feel when they do or say something that affects you in some way. You give them feedback. Of course, it works the other way around, as well. During the session or at another agreed-upon time, they give you feedback, too.

An effective feedback session follows certain tested guidelines: When you offer feedback, do so in an atmosphere of trust and caring, maintain a constructive tone, and remember that the goal of the discussion is to satisfy both parties' needs. The recipient must of course be willing to accept the feedback. As the recipient responds to your communication, you can employ the technique of paraphrasing to check your understanding of his or her remarks. To make it clear that you are criticizing only one aspect of the recipient's behavior and not his or her whole personality, be sure to mix positive and negative feedback appropriately.

Additional guidelines apply regarding the focus of your feedback: Emphasize your own thoughts, feelings, and needs rather than attempting to interpret the recipient's behavior. Deal with aspects of the recipient's behavior that are subject to his or her control, not ingrained personality traits. Focus on relatively recent behavior that you have experienced directly, as opposed to hearsay or ancient history. Examine only one issue per feedback session, and be specific in explaining how the behavior in question affects you. In the final analysis, you must recognize that any changes in behavior, as well as the nature of those changes, are the responsibility of the recipient of the feedback.

Following these rules should produce the results you're after when dealing with most of the people with whom you work or live. They usually care about you and your feelings; otherwise, they would have been long gone from your life, either because you would have walked out or because they would have pushed you out.

In order to get the result you're after, you must (1) identify that result yourself (*before* starting the session) and (2) explain the desired result to the other person. If you don't, your unfocused discussion of potentially sensitive issues could backfire, leaving you to deal with a number of distasteful outcomes—such as a fight between you and the other person, the other person's physical or emotional withdrawal from the encounter, or a failure on your part to state your position properly.

Make your objective clear at the beginning, in your opening remarks. Put the person at ease—letting him or her know that you're not looking for a fight, that you're looking for help in solving a problem and reducing stress. Lay out the ground rules (even if everyone knows them already), getting his or her commitment to follow them and to work out an equitable solution. I'll illustrate this with a little dramatization involving Donna and her boss, Ellen:

Donna: Thanks for meeting with me. It's important to me because I have a problem I don't think I can solve alone.

Ellen: Sounds grim. What's up?

Donna: It's not as grim as it sounds, but I need to let you know what's happening with the Electronics Industries account. I'm taking a lot of heat for things over which I've got no control, and there's a good chance that I'll have a big cost overrun on this—a lot of additional billings.

Ellen: Yep. That's as grim as it sounds.

| **Donna:** | If it's O.K. with you, I'd like to make this one of our feedback sessions. Follow all the rules. |
| **Ellen:** | Sure, that's fine. Let's do it. |

Fortunately for Donna, though Ellen had been angry over the situation, their relationship was good to begin with, and Ellen is a reasonable person. It would have been very different if Ellen had said: "You'd better not have a big cost overrun. Go on, get back to work and bring this project in the way you should."

After Donna told Ellen how she sees things and feels about them, she was prepared to hear Ellen's feedback, in turn. As with the process of offering feedback, you can *receive* feedback more effectively by following certain rules: Prepare for the feedback session by removing all physical and mental distractions and approaching the encounter with an open mind, disposed to accept potentially valuable (though perhaps unwelcome) information.

As the other person delivers his or her message, interject brief comments to acknowledge your understanding of both the content and feelings expressed in the other's message. You're under no obligation to take corrective action unless you feel it would be mutually beneficial to do so. If you agree that a change does seem warranted, conclude the feedback session by working with the other person to develop an action plan to which you're both committed.

Notice that the really important part of receiving feedback is your willingness to *listen*—to refrain from defending yourself, giving reasons, or retorting. The best way to listen is to attend to everything the other person is saying and to ask questions for clarification or show in some way that you understand.

Questions for clarification take two forms—open-ended and closed-ended. Open-ended questions can't be answered by a simple yes or no. They begin with *what, why, who, when, where,* and *how*—the questions good journalists ask.

Closed-ended questions can be answered by a simple yes or no. They seek verification or confirmation.

They begin with words such as *will you, can you, did you, is it,* and *are they*.

A simple nod of the head (a gatekeeper that encourages the other person to continue talking) shows that you understand. Putting the other person's ideas into your own words and checking to see if you stated his or her case properly (paraphrasing) does a much better job of it. Additionally, telling the other person what emotions or feelings you're picking up from him or her (mirroring) makes it clear that you understand those factors as well as the content of the message.

Let's look at another part of the feedback session. Donna said her piece. Her boss listened carefully, asked questions for clarification, and acknowledged Donna's feelings. Now it's Ellen's turn.

As you read along, notice my notations in brackets. They point out how Ellen and Donna follow the guidelines and use the communication techniques I just covered.

Ellen: You're pretty angry about the way the contract was written and the way costing priced the program. [*Mirroring*]

Donna: You bet I am.

Ellen: I have to agree that other people made the errors that have brought you the most grief. Bruce was too eager to make a sale, and Phil was pretty careless about signing a contract he didn't read too well. Costing seems to have been too hasty in what they did, as well. [*Paraphrasing*]

Donna: That's the situation, at least the way I see it.

Ellen: I think you're right, but to tell the truth, Donna, I don't understand why you took so long to do something about it.

Donna: What do you mean? [*Open-ended question*]

Ellen: You're only 30 days out from the program. You've had it for 25 days before this, and you're asserting yourself for the first time. I should have been brought in earlier.

Donna: You think I should've asked for your help before this. [*Paraphrase*]

Ellen: Don't you? [*Closed-ended question*]

Donna: Maybe.

Ellen: Why didn't you? [*Open-ended question*]

Donna: I thought I could handle it myself.

Ellen: I can understand that, but I think it was misguided. You let me get angry with you when I should've been angry with Bruce, Phil, and costing—all of whom should be working on these problems. Now we'd better put our heads together and decide what to do. What do you think we should do first? [*Open-ended question*]

The rest of the discussion is irrelevant. We're only interested in *how* Donna and Ellen conducted the session. They both wanted a way to resolve the problems in the Electronics Industries program. Together they worked out a plan that brought in all the others, as well. Once they made those decisions, they also talked about how to manage their relationship more effectively than they had.

Donna: I appreciate that you met with me. I regret not having done it sooner.

Ellen: I do, too. Listen, you're still pretty new with the company and need to get used to how we do things—and to me and how I do things. How do you feel about coming to me sooner in the future, at least to tell me exactly what's going on?

Donna: Don't worry, I will. I feel a whole lot better than when I came in here. Like tons have been lifted off my shoulders. Something else hit me while we were talking. I need to memorize that file the moment I get it. And I've learned that you mean it when you say the door's always open.

Ellen: Good, because I do mean it. And I learned something, too. You're a proud person, and you have a right to be. You're competent, you're good at what you do, but I think your pride can get you into trouble. I'd better check with you more often to see whether you need help. If you don't, I'll mind my own business, but if you do, I expect you to tell me when I ask. A deal?

Donna: It's a deal.

With her stress greatly reduced, Donna's back in control of her own life at work, and she exercised control over Ellen, as well, by asking her to follow the rules for feedback. Since those were rules Ellen had used before, the whole discussion worked to their mutual benefit.

That doesn't mean another kind of person would have agreed to follow them. You and everyone else where you work may be experiencing a lot of relationship-induced stress and not even know that these guidelines for effective feedback exist. You may have to introduce them, set things up properly, and get people to treat each other with mutual respect. This book's short enough. Why not get everyone in your group to read it?

O.K. Let's get back to Donna. That took care of some of her job-specific stress, but her overall work-related stress includes what's happening at home. Not only does she carry her unhappiness around with her (the whole person goes to work), affecting how well she does, the conflict she has with Stan generates a lot of guilt feelings, a lot of self-doubt.

She started asking herself: "Am I doing the right thing? Am I being selfish, thinking only about myself and what I want rather than about Stan and the girls? Even if I am getting control at the office, maybe I ought to quit, for their sake." That guilt could have cost her more than her job. It could have cost her the career she had worked so hard to create, and it could even have cost her her self-respect.

Before Donna reached that point, she sat down with Stan and reopened communication, leveled about her feelings, and asked for his help in making fair and honest decisions. They needed new and better ways of relating to each other. They needed to deal with the stresses between them before they could relieve their individual stress.

A feedback session that included a discussion of what they wanted for themselves out of their lives, as well as what they wanted from each other, put them back on the road to a happier marriage. When people don't know what they want for themselves and from one another, they drift aimlessly—and usually, they drift apart.

Chapter 7

Stress and Your Goals in Life

For a woman today, a career makes greater sense than it ever has. Most families require two incomes just to survive and to maintain a decent standard of living. And though few couples like to discuss early on what happens if they should divorce, it's a greater possibility now than ever before. Two out of three first marriages end in divorce. And breadwinners often die before their spouses.

A woman's career today satisfies more than an ego need. While a career may satisfy a need for self-fulfillment, just as it does for a man, it also gives a woman a greater sense of security knowing that if something happens to her marriage, she can take care of herself and her children. Dependency not only creates immediate emotional stress, it also stunts the dependent person's ability to cope with future economic realities and the emotional stresses they create.

On the other side of the coin, a great deal of a breadwinning family man's stress comes from the anxieties of providing for his family in the style to which they'd like to become accustomed—and the fear that there would be no one to take care of the family in the event of his death. Stan can reduce *his own* stress to some degree by encouraging Donna to have a career that brings income into the house now and prepares her for a real future possibility.

Don't let my case study mislead you. Remember, Donna's a composite of typical men and women undergoing ordinary, daily pressures. Most people react to the circumstances of their lives, rather than satisfy their own needs. Appropriate, flexible planning ends the stress reaction living produces. Both men and women have to practice self-management.

Self-management means getting control through goal-directed knowledge, which by definition implies the *setting of goals.* To get control, you have to set measurable, observable, realistic, and achievable tangible and intangible objectives in the seven dimensions of your life (which are listed in the sidebar on the following page).

The tangible goals include payoffs or targets you can experience with your senses—income; status at work, in the community, and at home; possessions; and so on. Intangible goals include payoffs that satisfy emotional needs (such as the need for love) and feelings (such as personal happiness). Tangible goals relate to all aspects of your physical life; intangible goals relate to all aspects of your spiritual or intellectual life. Though the two different types of goals aren't mutually exclusive, people often have difficulty integrating them.

Many people experience stress because their work life and their nonwork life don't mesh. They think they can hold them separate and apart, but that's unrealistic. Not only does the whole person go to work, the whole person returns home, as well. To integrate the different aspects of your life—to bridge the gap between working for a living and living—you need to evaluate what you're doing in terms of the aforementioned seven dimensions of your life.

Some tangible and intangible goals support one another, or support or lead to another. For example, career goals lead to financial goals. Some tangible goals lead to intangible ones, such as the feeling of self-satisfaction when you get a raise or a promotion. Some intangible goals lead to tangible ones, as when

---

The Seven Dimensions of Your Life

1. *Financial* (tangible): levels of income; the amount of money you want to earn at different stages of your life and over the course of your lifetime.
2. *Career* (tangible): the types of activities through which you want to earn your income and the status in your profession you want to achieve.
3. *Material goods* (tangible): the types of things you want to own (such as a house, automobiles, furniture, clothing).
4. *Family* (intangible): the kinds of relationships you want to have with your relatives (for example, your immediate family, your spouse).
5. *Social relations* (intangible): the kinds of relationships you want to have with people other than your family (such as with friends and acquaintances).
6. *Community relations* (intangible): the status you want to achieve where you live (for instance, to be an elected official or a volunteer leader in a church or synagogue).
7. *Personal values* (intangible): the quality of health that you want to maintain; the degree of literacy and awareness that you want to reach; the spiritual values that are important to you; the happiness you want to feel.

---

you go to school to learn something before you discover that the knowledge can help you get a raise or promotion.

On the other hand, you feel stress when two or more goals come into conflict with each other, as in Donna's case—family-relationship goals and career goals. Before she could discuss them with Stan, she had to sort out her personal priorities for herself, and he had to sort out his for himself. They had to set down for themselves, individually, what they want for themselves out of their lives and out of their work and out of each other. Then they could come together to discuss how to work out the conflicts.

If you're having life-goal-related stress, you can do what Donna and Stan have done. A questionnaire in Appendix B (called "What Drives You?") will help you identify your most important goals, the payoffs that drive you at this time. Your identified payoffs may change over time, but, then, what doesn't change? Doing the exercise periodically helps you set priorities regularly. Then you can communicate them to the significant others in your world.

Well-formulated goal statements contain *targets* (for example, "earn $35,000 a year"). They include *deadlines* (for example, "by the end of this year"). They specify the *conditions* under which you will reach the target, both the means and the contingencies (for example, "by managing the programs assigned to me with a minimum of a 10 percent margin and by setting up a communication system with costing that will eliminate the underpricing we've had"). Pulling together the example, a well-formulated goal statement looks like this:

> *Earn $35,000 a year by the end of this year, by managing the programs assigned to me with a minimum of a 10 percent margin and by setting up a communication system with costing that will eliminate the underpricing we've had.*

You then take the list of conditions and turn them into goal statements, as well:

> *By the end of the month, work out a communication system with costing that will eliminate the underpricing we've had by meeting with Ellen and the costing-department supervisor, by setting new policies . . .*

Each such goal statement is an objective, a milestone toward accomplishing the goal from which you derive the objective. This is how you eat an elephant—one bite at a time.

Break up the large goal into smaller, achievable goals. You feel you're getting somewhere when you achieve predetermined milestones. You feel in control, and the feelings of success reduce stress.

By setting up a plan for your life, you prepare yourself for dealing with obstacles, few of which are unexpected. If you do what-if planning, you take the stress out of encountering barriers. "What if Stan won't back away from his feelings about my work? I may be forced to leave him, or I can change my job, or I can get him to agree to family counseling, or . . ."

With a plan, you can evaluate each alternative for its appropriateness and feasibility. Without a plan, you can only react to whatever comes your way—and feel stress.

Sometimes, even with a plan, it seems that life is out of control, that you're not getting anywhere, or that you're inadequate to the task of achieving your own goals. Then you need a first aid device to regain control of your own feelings and thoughts.

For the most part, you are what you think you are, you can do what you believe you can do. One thing's for sure. You can never be what you want to be, you can never achieve what you want for yourself, if you believe that you *can't*. When you believe you can't or feel bad about yourself, you need to get yourself out of that negative frame of mind and back into a positive one. You're only stressing yourself with negative thoughts or feelings.

On a day when you're feeling good about yourself, make a bragging list. Boast. List all your personal strengths and virtues. For example, "I'm very good at getting people to work with me." List all your accomplishments. For example, "I brought in the Smith program at 15 percent under, and the client wrote a very positive letter about me to Ellen." Let yourself go. List *everything* you like about yourself. No one else will ever make that list for you.

A lot of people feel odd about making a bragging list. They've been taught it's not nice to brag. Let other people tell you how good you are. That piece of advice has inhibited people from telling *themselves* how good they are.

But I'm not telling you to brag to other people. I'm

telling you to brag to yourself. It's your reminder to yourself that you're competent, capable, strong, healthy—all the good things you like about yourself. What's so bad about that?

Record the list on an audiocassette, one you can play to yourself when you need it. It's another form of self-talk.

Instead of listening to some professional motivator tell you—and everyone else to whom he or she has sold the tape—how wonderful you are, tell yourself. You know yourself better than the professional does, and you need to believe in yourself as you are and want to be, not as the professional motivator thinks you should be. It's your life. Get control over it yourself and motivate yourself to keep control.

Conclusion

Pulling Your Controls Together

No one can eliminate or avoid stress altogether. It's your body's way of preparing to protect itself from danger by fighting against it or by fleeing from it. It's your mind's interpretation of what's happening in your life—it's good (Eustress), or it's bad (Distress).

You want to repeat experiences of Eustress because they make you feel good. You want to repeat some kinds of Distress because they motivate you to achieve your own goals or the goals of the organization to which you belong and with which you want to remain. Rather than eliminate or avoid stress altogether, practice the self-management skills described in this book in order to manage your stress and the conditions that induce it.

The stress of a situation comes from your reaction to

it. How you interpret your experiences includes your stress reactions to them. Everyone experiences events they interpret as threatening, and it's your ability, or lack of it, to cope with them and with your reactions to them that generates the stress. The less in control of events you feel, the more stress you feel.

Managing stress requires you to identify what feelings you have, and when, and under what conditions. Once you have that information, you can take steps to reduce or manage the stress or the conditions that induce it.

A popular prayer comes to mind:

Lord, grant me the strength to change the things I can; the serenity to accept those I can't; and the wisdom to know the difference.

You can't change the conditions that induce stress as readily as you can change your responses to them. When you achieve the wisdom to know what you can and can't change, you'll find the serenity you need for taking corrective action with regard to the conditions. Part of that serenity comes from putting the ordinary pressures of daily life into perspective by comparing them with the one thing you dread the very most. Nothing else can induce as much stress as the thought of that.

First aid exercises or activities give temporary relief. Those first aid measures, however, don't give you control over the conditions that induce the stress.

Develop action plans for getting control over the stress-causing conditions. Whatever disturbs you—the physical environment or your interpersonal relations or your own life situation—take corrective action. The worst course of action when feeling stress is to do nothing at all. Changing the environment, working out problems with other people, planning for your own life all involve some element of risk—which induces different types of stress—but unless you take that risk, you're jeopardizing your life.

Appendix A

Script for
Talking Away Your Stress

Instructions

(1) Fill in the blanks (in parentheses) in the script with scenes or ideas appropriate to yourself or choose the options that best fit you. (2) Practice reading the script several times before turning on the recorder. (3) Read into the recorder, speaking softly and slowly. Play soft music in the background if you wish. If you make mistakes, don't worry, you're the only one who's going to hear them. (4) Play the tape back to yourself with a critical ear. If you like what you hear, use the tape as is. If you don't like it, do it again, or if you can, rerecord the part you don't like and edit the tape. (5) You'll find additional italicized instructions placed in brackets in the script itself.

Script

Relax. You will not fall asleep. You are just going to make yourself comfortable (in your chair) (on your bed) (on the floor).

Give yourself permission to relax. When I tell you to inhale, take a deep breath to signal your body and your brain that you want to relax. While you're holding your breath, I'll count to five, after which you can exhale, also to a slow count of five.

Adapted from Donald H. Weiss, *Talk Away Your Stress,* an audiocassette produced by Self-Management Associates, Dallas, Texas (1982).

Inhale. One—two—three—four—five.

Exhale. One—two—three—four—five.

Now you're beginning to relax. The tension is leaving all your muscles, and your mind is starting to focus on relaxing. On nothing else. On nothing but relaxing.

Focus on a spot directly in front of your eyes. Stare at it, and if your eyelids feel heavy and begin to close, let them.

While staring at the spot, focus your mind on your own breathing. Breathe in naturally, and breathe out naturally. Don't try to regulate it. Listen to the natural rhythm of your breathing. Say the words to yourself as you breathe: "Breathe in. Breathe out." Focus on the natural pattern of your breathing.

Feel your eyelids getting heavy. Let them close on their own, shutting out the light, relaxing your eyes as you listen to your breathing and become more and more relaxed.

With your eyes closed, feel the air entering your nostrils, passing through your nose. Feel and hear yourself breathing in and out, and enjoy the pleasure of being alive. A living human being full of hopes and dreams, full of joy and love.

On your own now, listen to your breathing. (Lie there) (Sit in your chair) and listen to yourself inhaling and exhaling.

[Pause for 20 seconds. Begin again, speaking even softer than you did before.]

You're beginning to feel very relaxed. Relax your jaw. Let it fall (slack *[if you're lying down]*) (open *[if you're sitting]*). You're going to take an imaginary walk.

You're going to walk out _____. See _____ in your mind's eye. See the _____. Feel the warm sun. Feel it soak into your body. Feel the gentle breeze caress your skin, your arms, your face.

It feels so good to stand there in the warm sun. It feels so good that you walk on farther _____, to a place where you can lie down. Feel the _____ cushioning you as you lie there, with it forming a soft bed for your back, your hips, your legs, and your head.

44

How pleasant it is to lie there in the warm sun, listening to the _____ calling out their love songs to one another.

Feel the breeze, feel the warm sun, feel the _____ on which you're lying. Watch the puffy white clouds sail silently across the sky. Relax. Rest. As you relax, focus your mind on the top of your head. Let your scalp relax. Smooth the wrinkles from your forehead, and remove the tension on the top of your head. Let your head (rest on the surface) (bow loosely; don't force it erect). Take the burden from the back of your neck.

Focus on the back of your neck. Let the muscles unwind, and let (your head and neck rest against the surface) (your chin rest against your chest). As your neck loosens, let the skin on your face soften and sag. Focus your mind on it. Smooth out all the wrinkles around your eyes and around your mouth. Keep your jaw relaxed.

Now focus on your shoulders. Let your shoulders relax (falling back against the surface) (just hanging loosely from your spine). Feel all the tension in your head, neck, and shoulders flow down through your arms as you let the muscles of your arms relax and hang. All the way to your fingers, tension flows down your arms and out through your fingertips. Your arms hang loosely by your sides, at one with the (surface on which you lie) (chair on which you sit).

With your head, neck, shoulders, arms, and fingers relaxed, with all the tension gone from them, focus on your back. Let your back relax. From your shoulders to the small of your back, feel the muscles (flatten out against the surface) (sag against the back of the chair). ([*Add the following if you're sitting.*] Your head moves forward even a little more as your body responds to gravity's gentle pull.)

It feels so good to rest your back, so now focus your mind on your chest. Rest your rib cage, letting your lungs breathe naturally as you feel your rib cage ease gently (backward toward the surface) (forward toward your knees). Feel all the tension ease out of your upper body, and in your mind's eye, feel the warm sun on your face, the _____ under your back, and hear _____.

Rest as you let your stomach relax. Focus on the muscles of your midsection and feel the center of your body relax. And as you relax, feel your hips and pelvis also go slack against (the surface) (the back of the chair). Focus on them and loosen them up.

Rest also as you focus on the muscles of your thighs. Give your tired and tense muscles permission to rest.

Let the tension flow out of your abdomen, down your hips and down your thighs toward your calves. Concentrate on the calves. Relax the muscles in them. Let them go limp. Let the (surface) (floor) support them. Let the tension flow right down to your toes and out and away.

It feels so good to let go, to let all your muscles relax, and to let your mind focus on nothing but relaxing as the tension flows out of your body.

It feels so good to lie _____ with _____ beneath your back, the sun warming your face, the soft breeze on your skin. Watch the clouds. Listen to _____. Quiet. Relaxed. Gentle. Easy.

Listen to your breathing again. Listen to your breathing as you (lie) (sit) quietly, letting your body and your mind feel the pleasure and contentment of being completely and totally relaxed. Focus on how good it feels to be so relaxed. Fix in your mind how every muscle feels as you relax. Know what you should feel every time you want to relax. While feeling relaxed, you're in control. Nothing around you or within you can bother you. You are in repose. Your feelings are under your control. You are relaxed and in control.

But now it's time to return from your walk out _____. It's time to leave the _____, the _____, the warm sun, the gentle breeze, and the clouds. I'll count slowly, and when I reach ten, gradually open your eyes. Don't come out of your relaxed state all at once, but instead, take a few moments to savor the way you feel. One—two—three—four—five—six—seven—eight—nine—ten.

Slowly open your eyes. *[Pause for five seconds.]* Slowly (sit up) (raise your head). Sit quietly for a few seconds before moving about. Feel the gentle muscle tone all over your body. Keep the feeling in your mind. Notice the slow regularity of your breathing. Keep that feeling in your mind, as well. Bask in the good feeling of being relaxed. Remember how it feels. Whenever your muscles tighten, whenever you experience stress, recall those tranquil feelings and recapture them.

Turn off the player now, and (go to sleep) (go about your business) feeling relaxed.

[End of tape]

Appendix B

What Drives You?

Anything you do, you do for a reason, even if you don't know what that reason is. Every action produces an end result, and unless you plan for it, the end result you get may not satisfy the reason for which you took the action in the first place.

Some reasons compel you more than others. We call them motives, and we can trace them back to needs or wants. The reasons that motivate most forcefully are your drivers—your most important reasons for doing what you're doing. Satisfying those drivers becomes your highest-priority activity because reaching those goals means getting the payoffs you want for yourself. So what are your drivers?

The list below consists of 25 possible reasons for

Adapted from Donald H. Weiss, *Getting Results: The Performance Appraisal Process,* a cassette/workbook program (New York: American Management Association, 1985).

doing anything. Each word or phrase can be used to answer the question, "What do I want to get out of the effort I'm putting into my life?"

Step 1

This is important. Read the *entire* list of possible payoffs *before* continuing. *Stop here* and read the list.

_____ 1. *Knowledge:* To pursue and learn about new things and ideas; to search for truth or information; to be known by others as an intelligent person and feel intelligent.

_____ 2. *Wisdom:* To understand and shape for myself a meaning of life, perceiving experience from a broad frame of reference.

_____ 3. *Power:* To lead and direct others; to influence or control others—that is, to get them to do what I want them to do.

_____ 4. *Aesthetic Pleasure:* To enjoy and respect the things from which I derive pleasure—art, nature, work, people.

_____ 5. *Ethical standards:* To believe in and maintain a code of ethics, a sense of right and wrong; to be moral; to conform to the standards of society, my family or spouse, my profession, and my personal or religious ideals.

_____ 6. *Independence:* To achieve my own goals in the manner best suited to me; to have the freedom to come and go as I wish; to be myself at all times; to control my own actions.

_____ 7. *Accomplishment:* To achieve my personal objectives with a sense that I've down something as well as, if not better than, someone else would have; to experience self-satisfaction when I rise to a challenge, accomplish a task or a job, or solve a problem.

_____ 8. *Recognition:* To receive attention, notice, approval, or respect from others because of something I've done; to generate a positive feeling in others for who I am and what I achieve.

_____ 9. *Friendship:* To have many friends; to work with others, enjoying their camaraderie; to join groups for companionship; to look forward to and enjoy social relations.

_____ 10. *Responsibility:* To be held accountable to others or to organizations to which I belong for a job or task; to possess something and care for it.

_____ 11. *Creativity:* To be true to, and have the ability and desire to, develop new ideas, solutions to problems, improvements in products or procedures, or designs or plans; to be mentally challenged; to be the first to innovate or create.

_____ 12. *Security:* To possess the basic wherewithal for living; to feel safe; to have self-confidence; to have job security and continuity of income.

_____ 13. *Dedication:* To be loyal to the company or my supervisor, my family, social and political groups, and others; to give devotion, commitment, or friendship to others.

_____ 14. *Justice and Parity:* To receive rewards and recognition for my contributions and achievements in proportion to my effort and comparable to those received by other people.

_____ 15. *Growth:* To advance, to expand my life through my job, through the improvement of my status at work or in the community; to increase my work-related and non-work-related knowledge or skill; to find fulfillment in the groups in which I work or live; to mature personally and professionally.

_____ 16. *Self-esteem:* To be someone of value in my own eyes and in the eyes of other people; to be accepted as a person rather than as a nonentity or as a means to an end; to feel useful and wanted by other people; to be a leader; to be appreciated by others.

_____ 17. *Religiousness:* To believe in a supreme being; to relate to others on a spiritual or personal basis with respect to some faith or set of beliefs.

_____ 18. *Love:* To experience warmth, feelings of affection, a sense of caring, enthusiasm for, attachment to, devotion to, and interest in something or another person, especially someone to whom I can make a commitment.

_____ 19. *Challenge:* To feel good about what I do, its degree of difficulty, and its complexity or demands on my creativity; to have opportunities to apply my knowledge and skills effectively and easily.

_____ 20. *Faith:* To have self-confidence and to believe in my abilities and skills, in the goodness and value of life, and in the goals and objectives of my company or social organizations; to feel secure in the availability of help from others and to recognize help received.

_____ 21. *Helpfulness:* To provide assistance, support, empathy, or protection to others; to be open, responsive, and generous.

_____ 22. *Health (physical/mental):* To feel energetic and free of physical pain from injury, disease, or infection; to feel free of worry and anxiety and of emotional blocks to success in all aspects of my life; to have peace of mind.

_____ 23. *Money:* To have sufficient income or other assets to use as I wish; to be materially comfortable or well-off.

    24. *Good times/pleasure:* To have fun; to enjoy myself; to do things I like to do rather than only things I have to do.

    25. *Being loved:* To experience warmth, feelings of affection, and a sense of caring from other people, especially from someone from whom I can expect a commitment.

Step 2

Return to the beginning of the list. Slowly review each item, *ranking* each payoff as to its *importance to you.* In the spaces provided, write *1* for the most important and up to *25* for the least. For example, if you feel that *knowledge* is an important reason for doing things but not the most important, you might write an *8* on the line next to the first item on the list. It may make things easier if you hunt out the item that represents the most important reason before you rate the rest.

Turn to steps 3 and 4 only after you have finished step 2.

Step 3

From your master list, transfer the top five payoffs you want from your *work* to the accompanying chart. For example, you could list *recognition* as the most important work-related driver, even if it ranks lower than that on your master list.

Step 4

List the five *personal* payoffs you want to satisfy outside the workplace. These drivers help you maintain your psychological well-being and your social relationships.

Notes: Use the example as a guide. When you complete the list of payoffs in each group, compare those lists with each other. Note which side of the chart

EXAMPLE

Rank	Work-related Drivers	Rank	Non-work-related Drivers
2	Recognition	1	Love
4	Friendship	3	Being loved
5	Accomplishment	4	Friendship
15	Money	20	Religiousness
9	Responsibility	8	Aesthetic pleasure

YOUR LIST OF DRIVERS

Rank	Work-related Drivers	Rank	Non-work-related Drivers

contains the highest ratings in the master list—work-related or non-work-related.

In some cases, payoffs may be both work-related and non-work-related. For example, many people seek *friendship* at work as well as outside of work. The example shows that you can list a driver on both sides of the chart.

When you finish, you'll have a personal profile, a picture of your own most important motives or reasons for doing things. If you're experiencing stress, check your lists of payoffs to see which of them you're *not* getting. The frustration of not getting that payoff (or those payoffs) may be a cause of the stress you're feeling.

INDEX

ABOUT THE AUTHOR

Donald H. Weiss, Ph.D., of Millers' Mutual Insurance in Alton, Illinois, has been engaged in education and training for over 26 years and has written numerous articles, books, audio cassette/workbook programs, and video training films on effective sales and supervisory or management skills. He speaks regularly on stress management and other personal development subjects, and has produced a variety of related printed or recorded materials.

During his career, Dr. Weiss has been the Manager of Special Projects for a training and development firm, the Manager of Management Training for an insurance company, the Director of Training for an employment agency group, a training consultant, and a writer-producer-director of video training tapes. He also has taught at several universities and colleges in Texas, including the University of Texas at Arlington and Texas Christian University, in Fort Worth.

Currently, Dr. Weiss is Corporate Training Director for Millers' Mutual Insurance.